DOT MARKER BOOK BELONGS TO

____

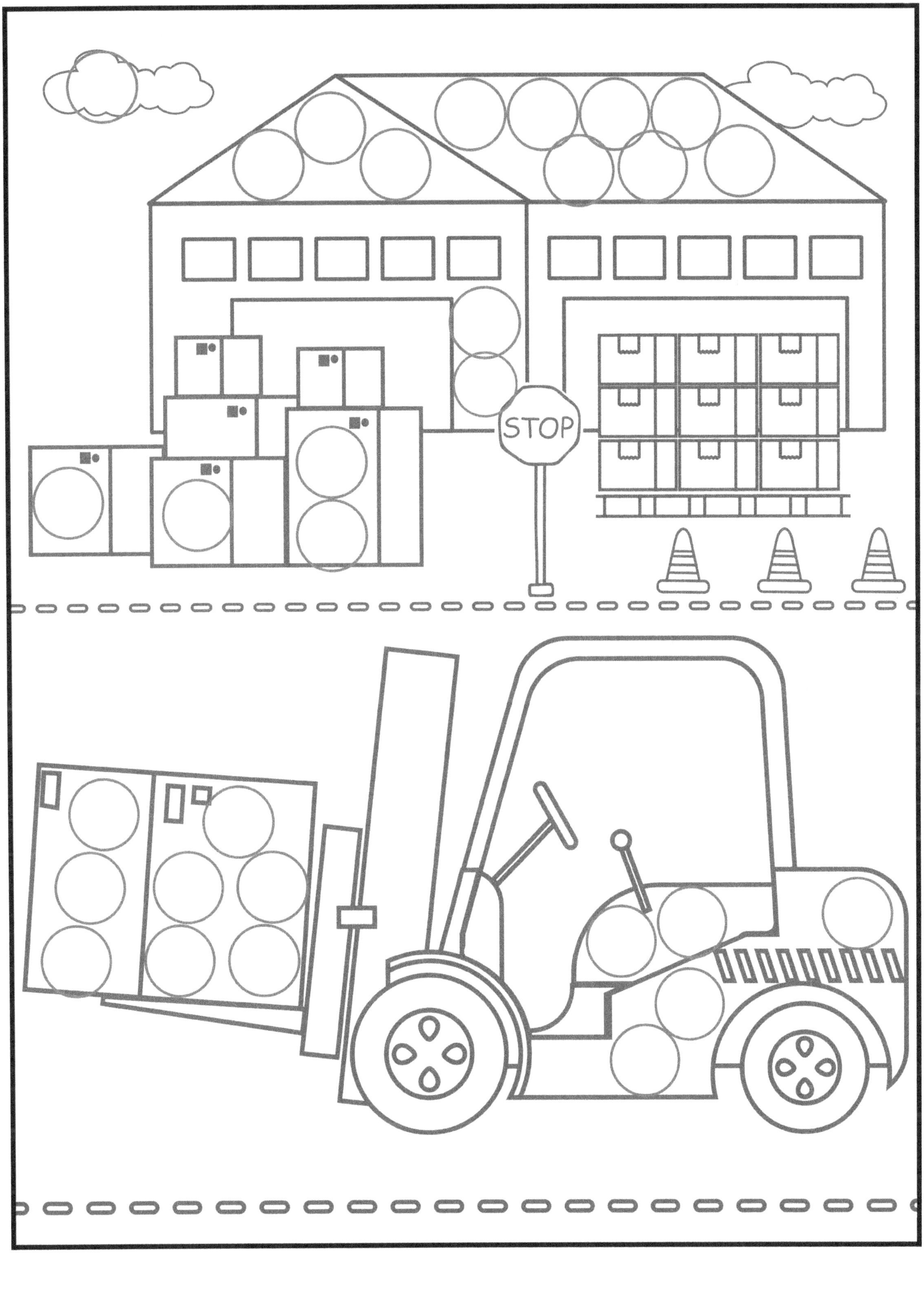
STOP

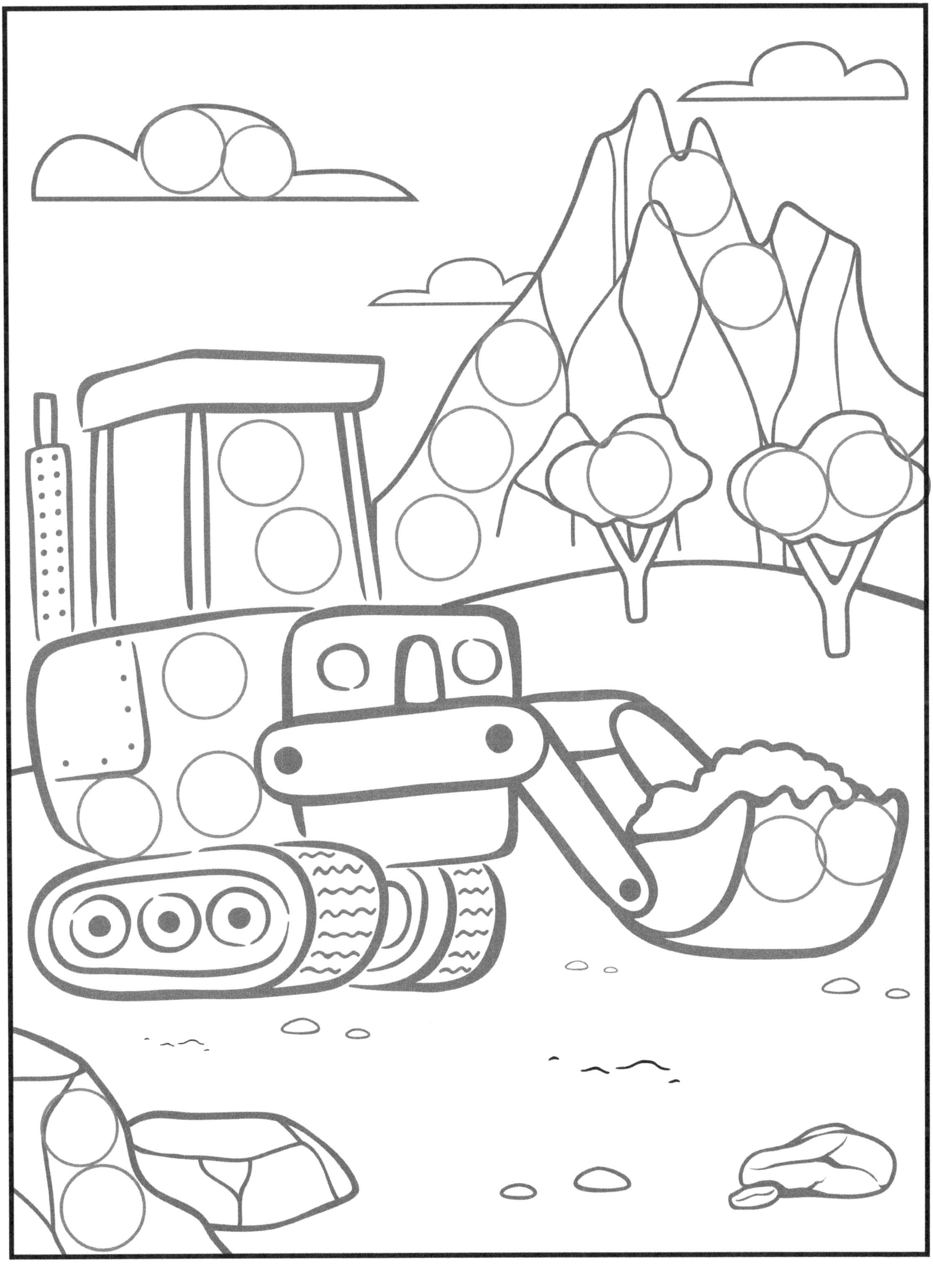

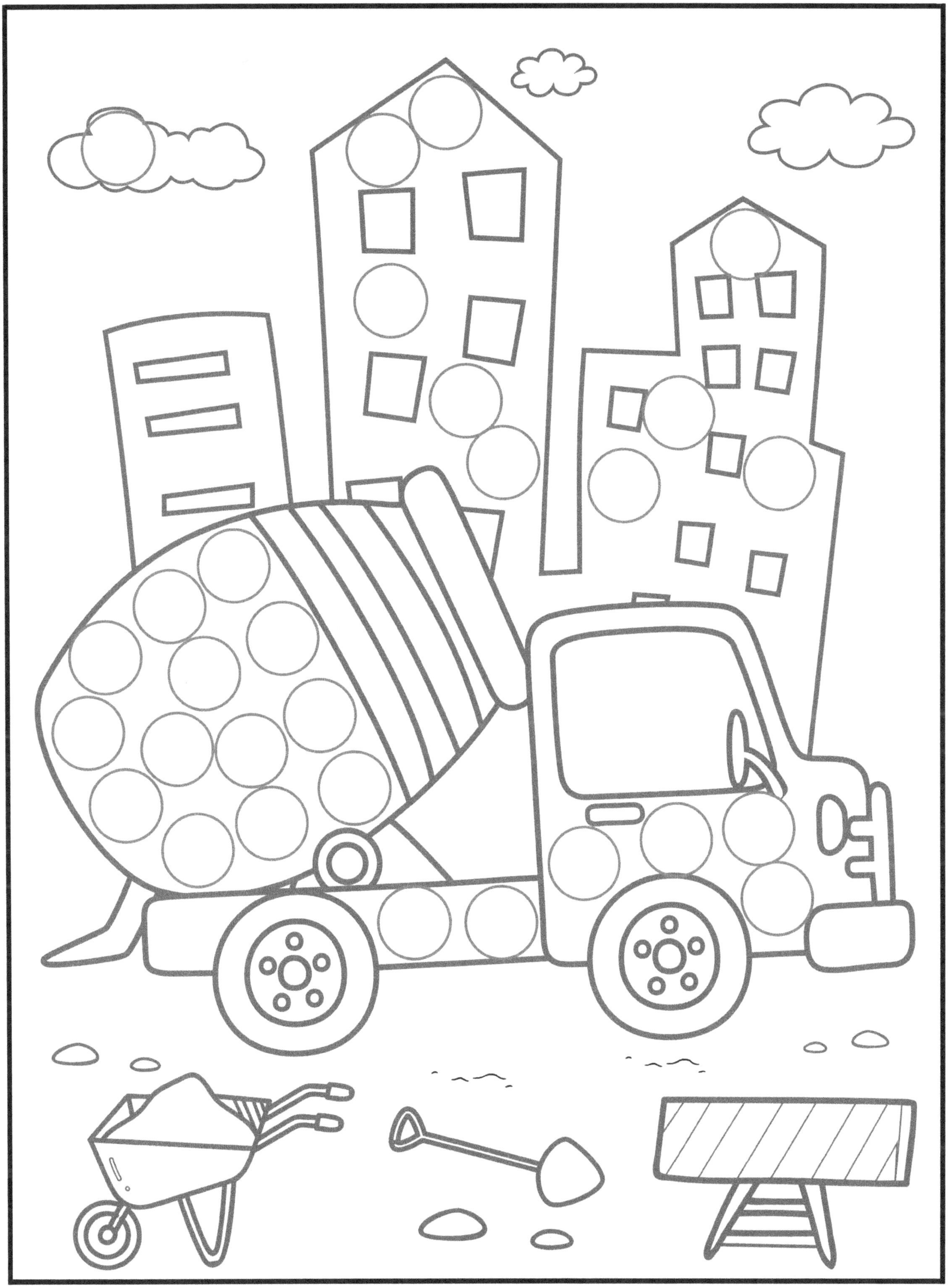

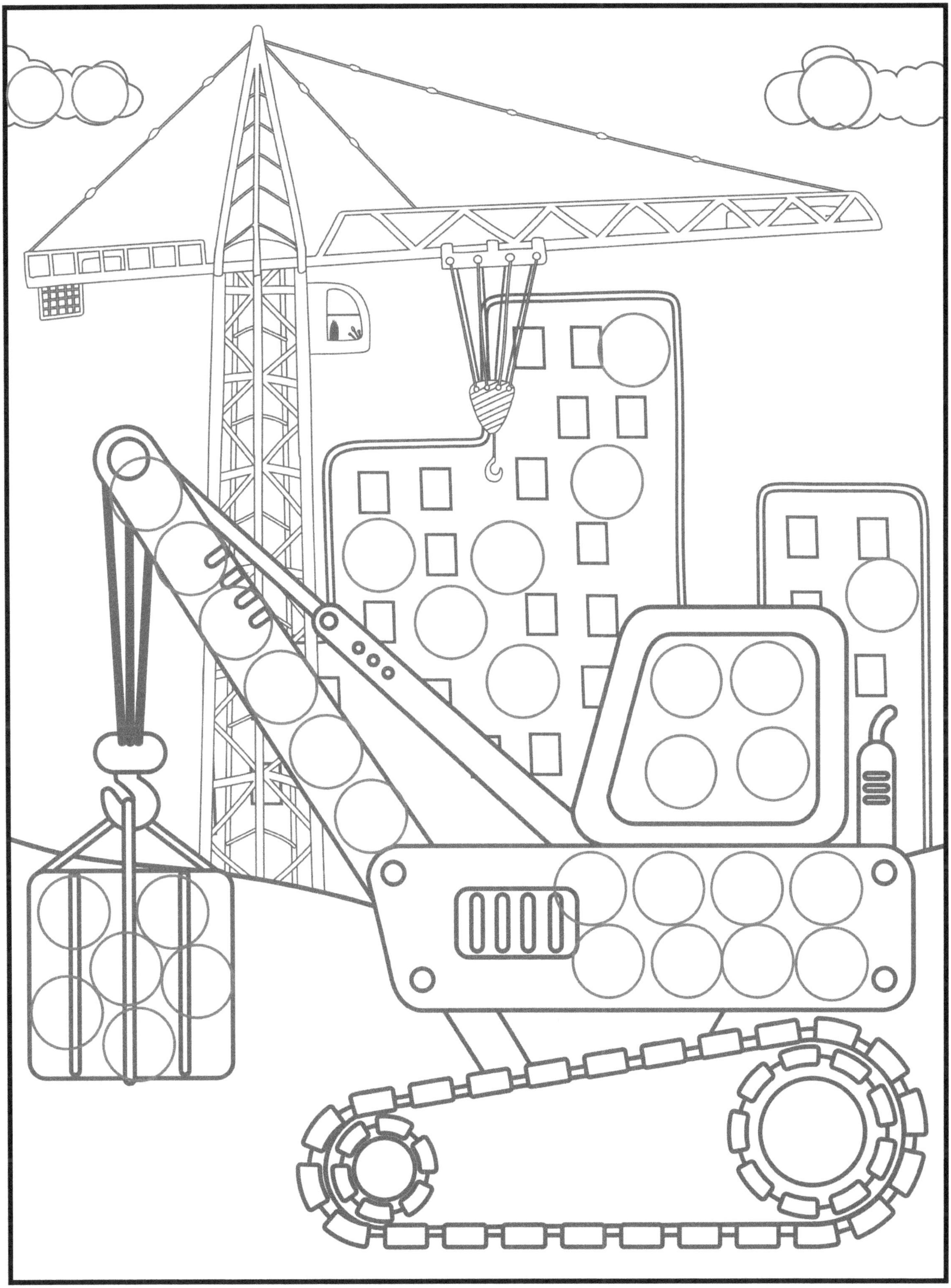

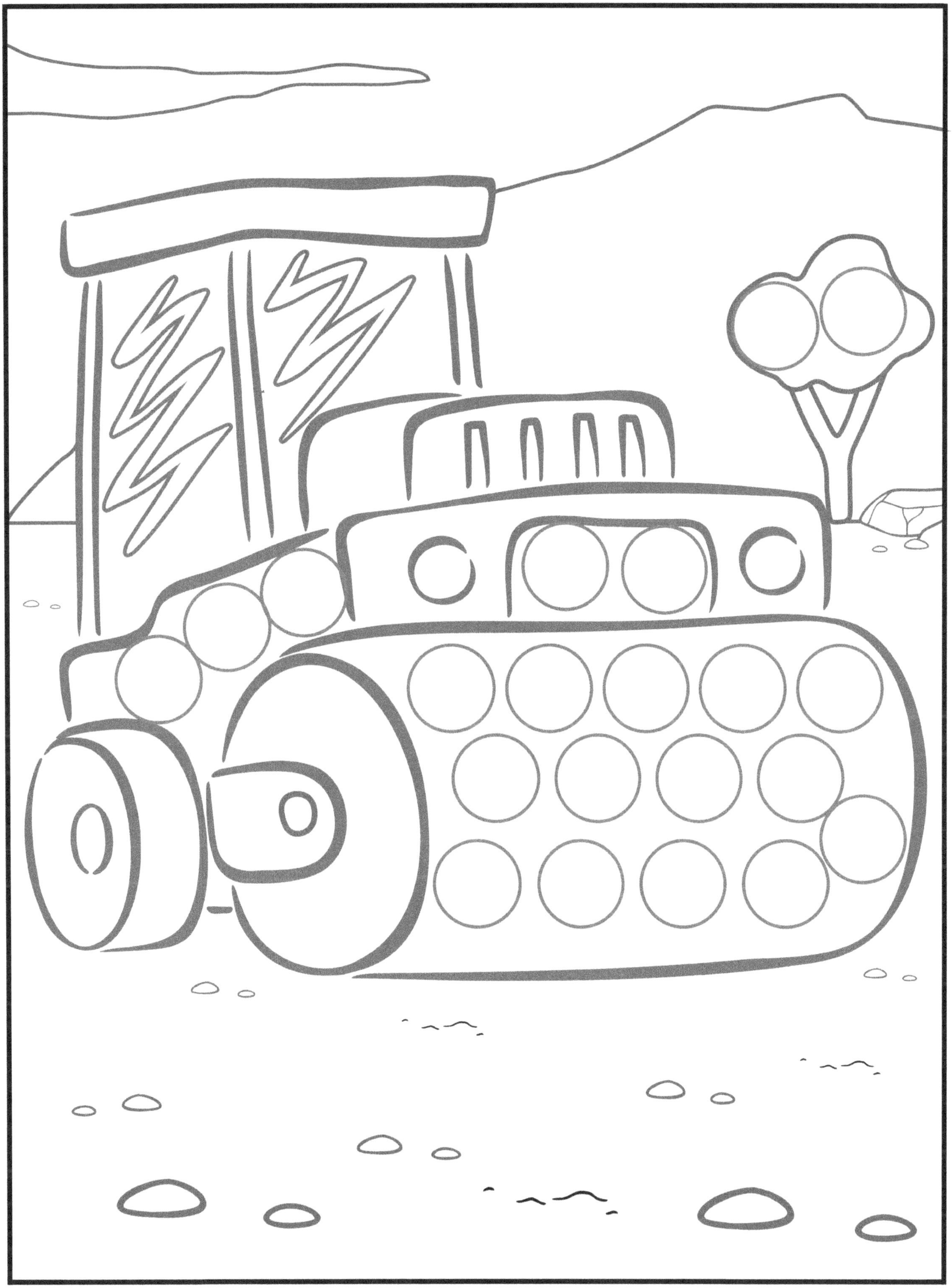

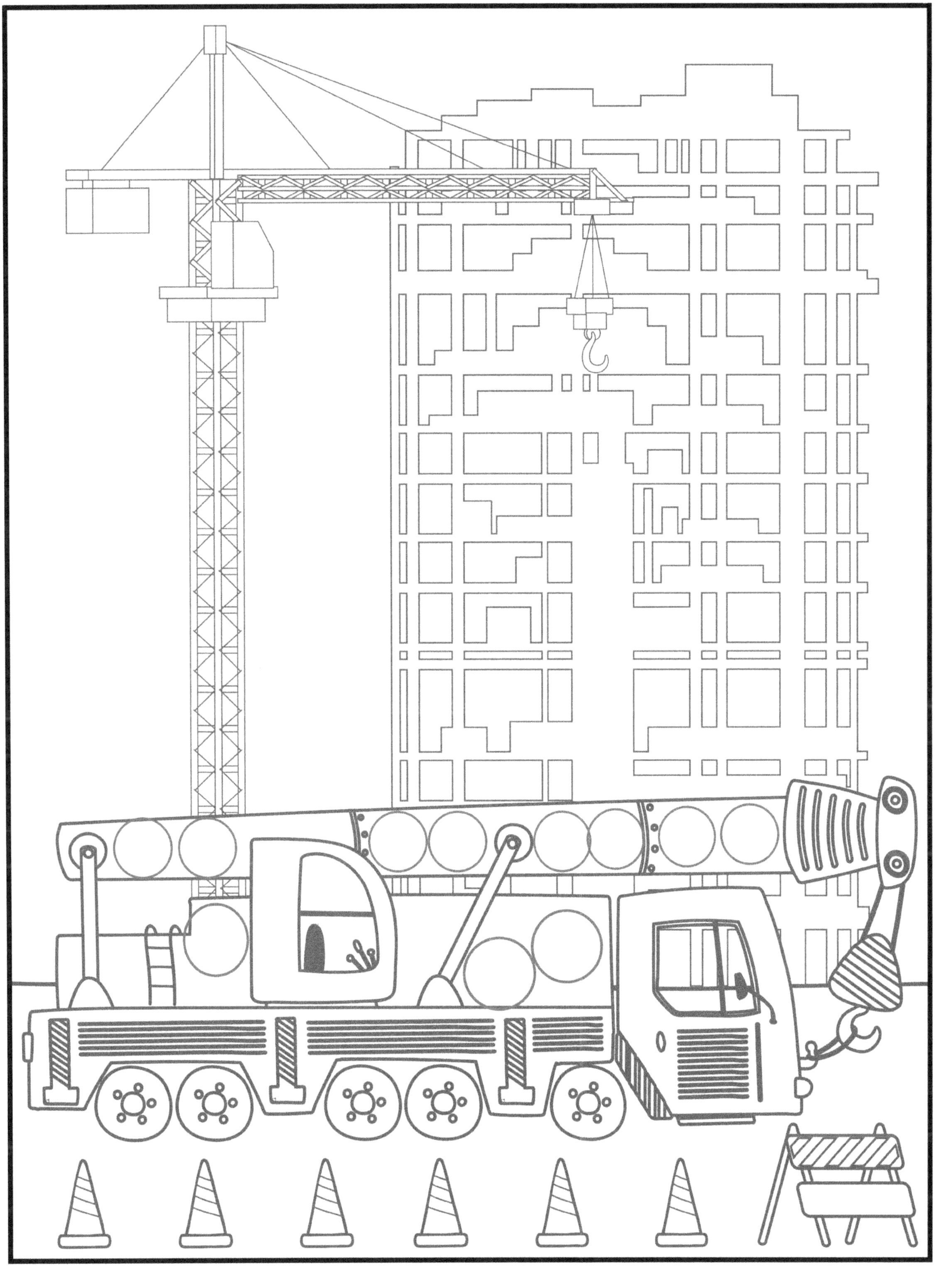

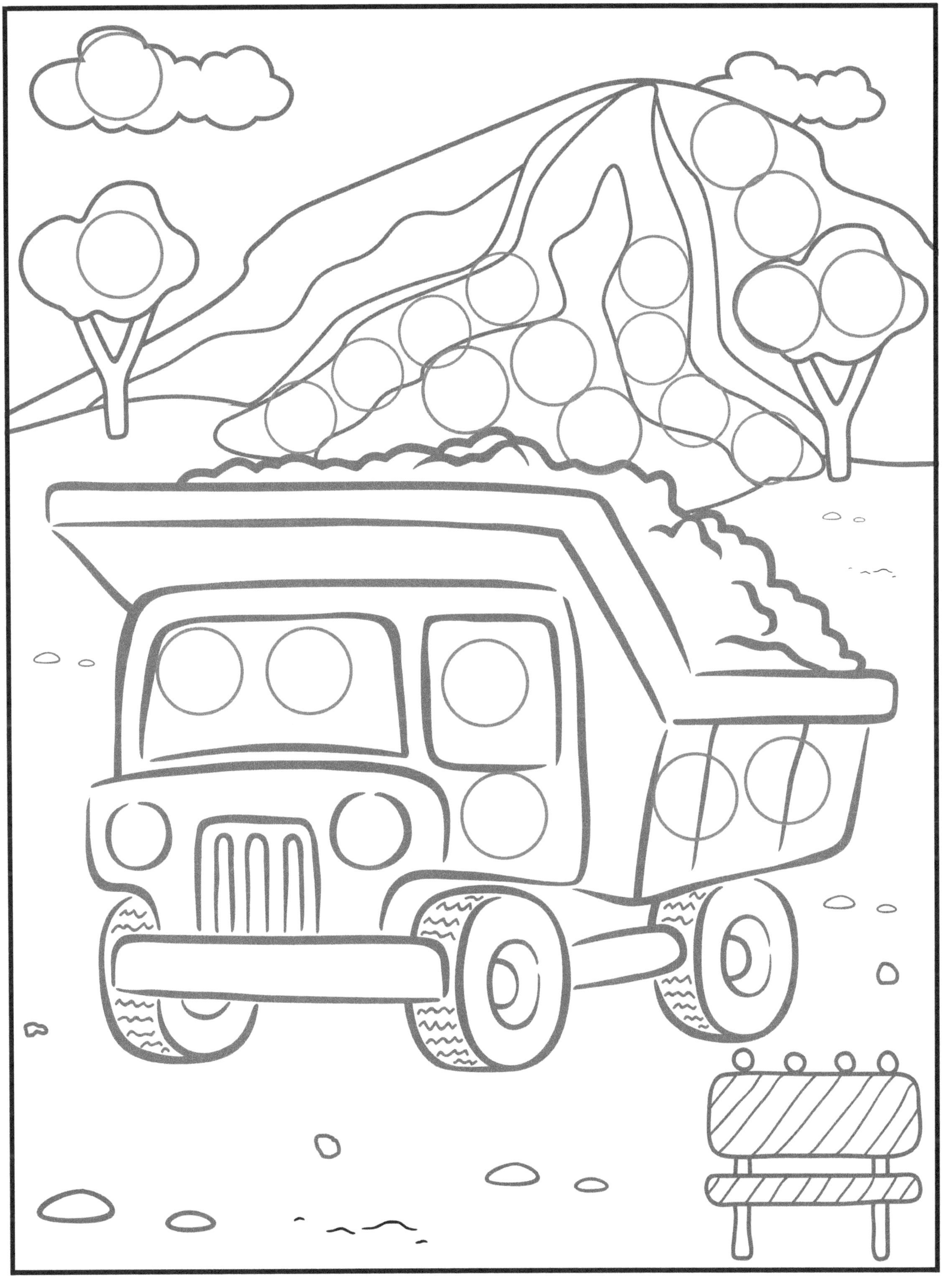

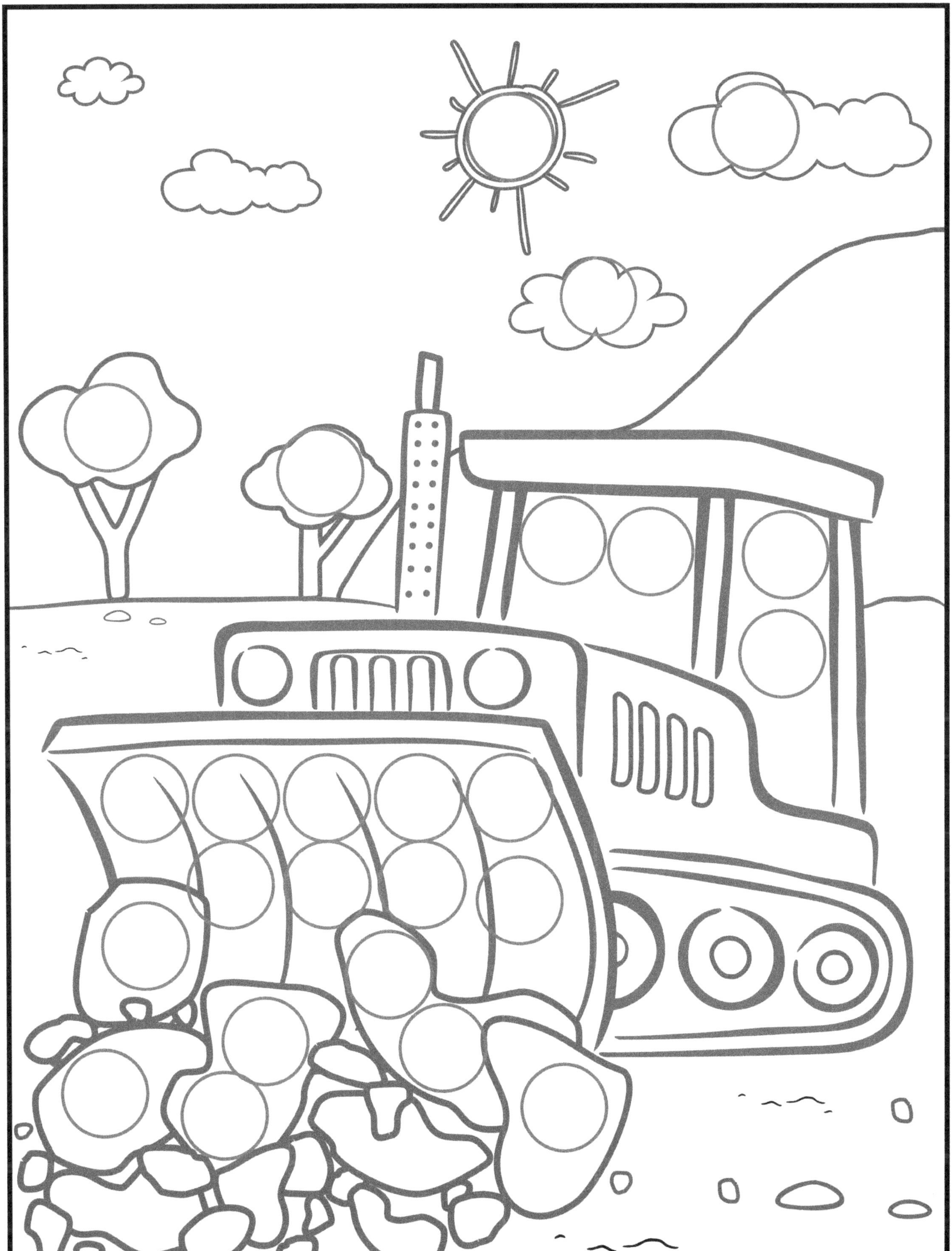

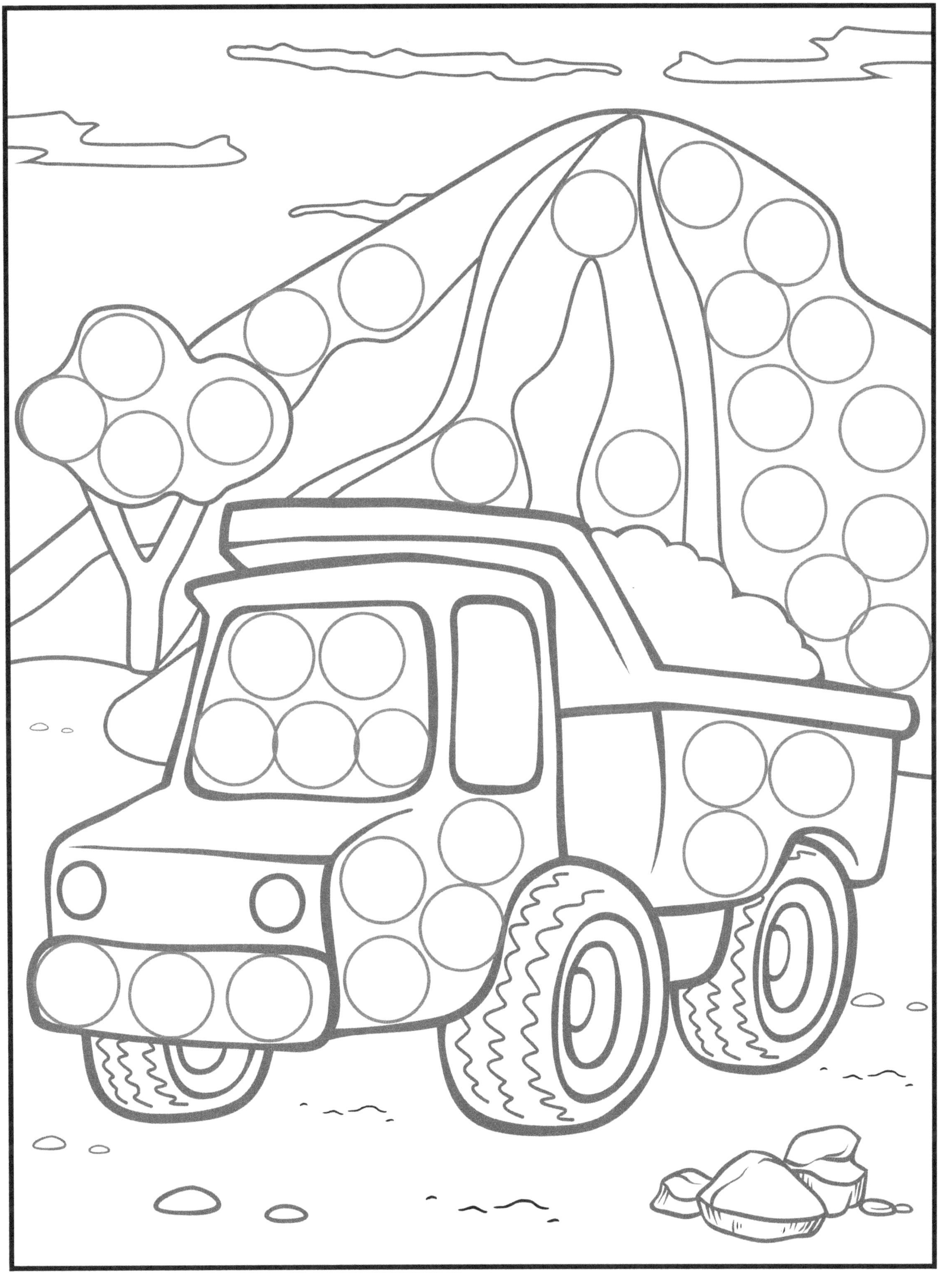

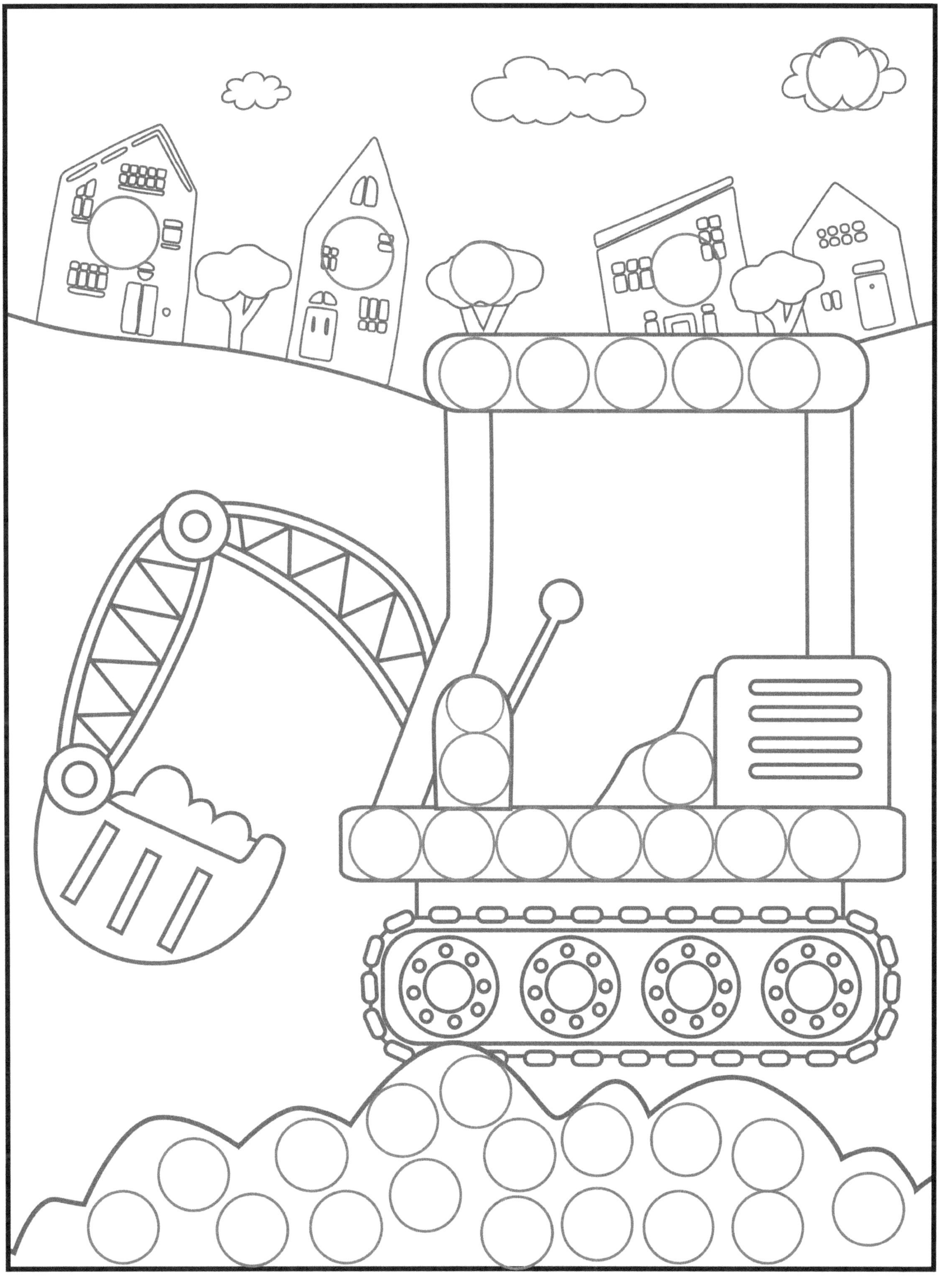

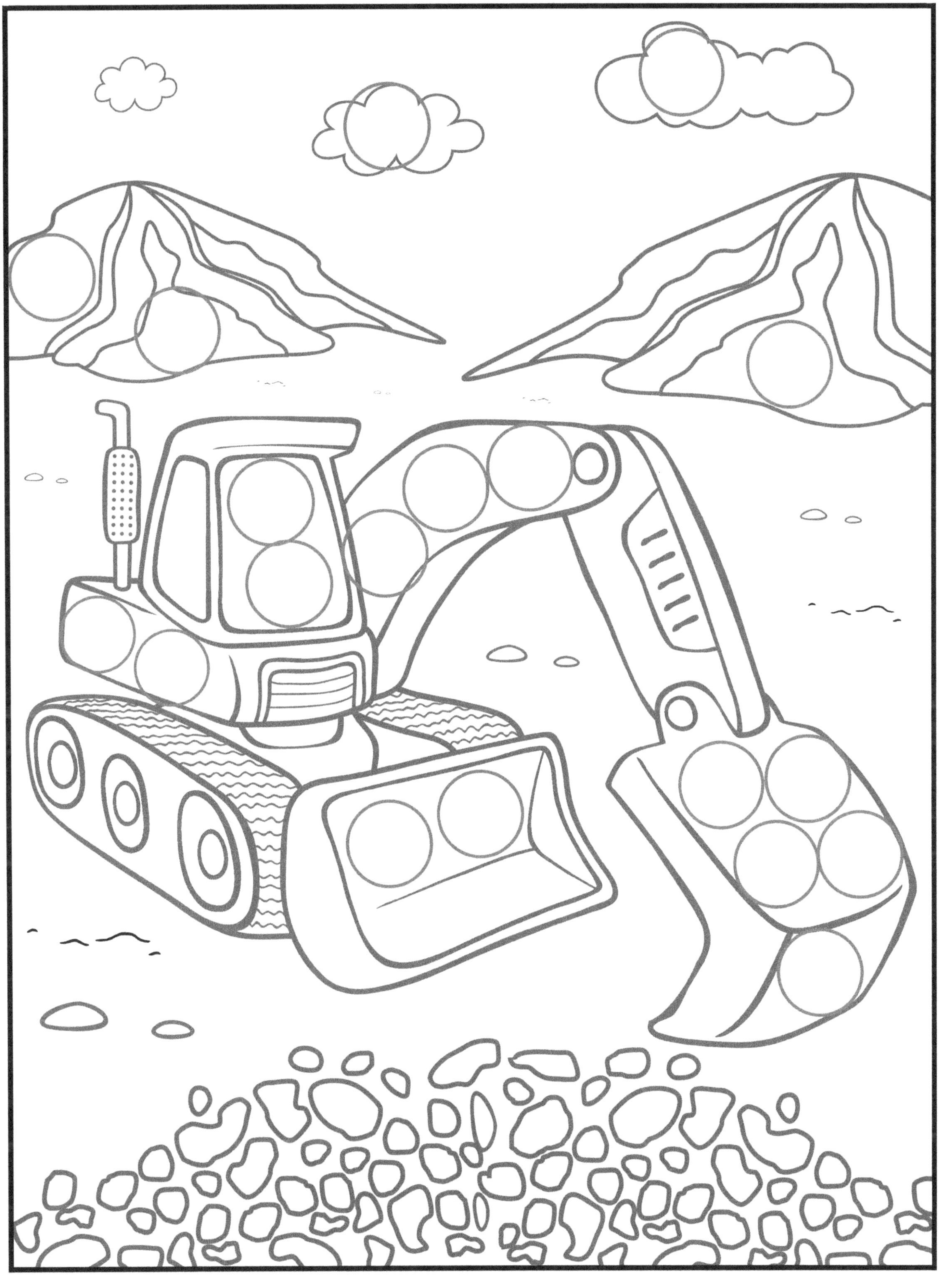

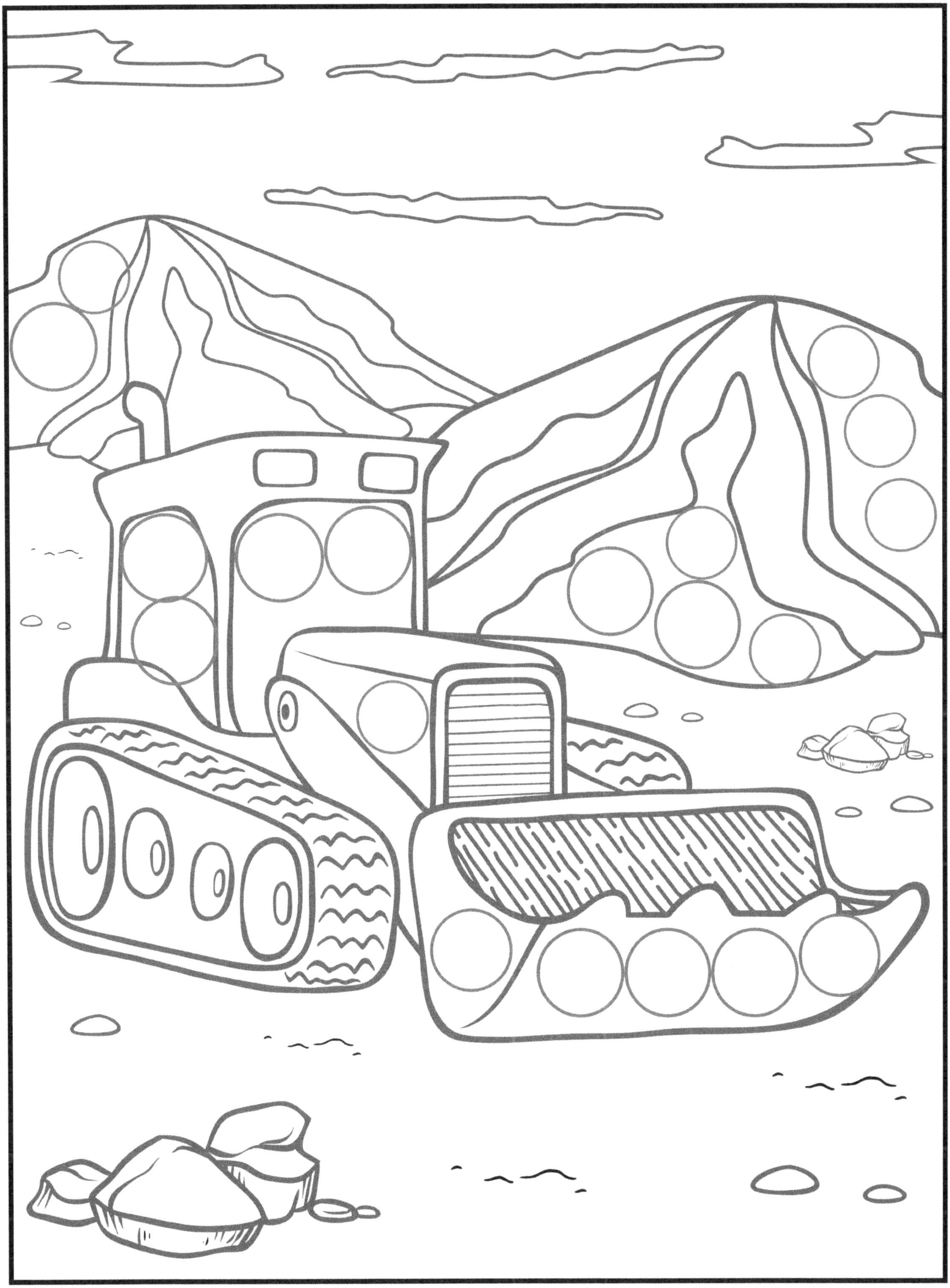

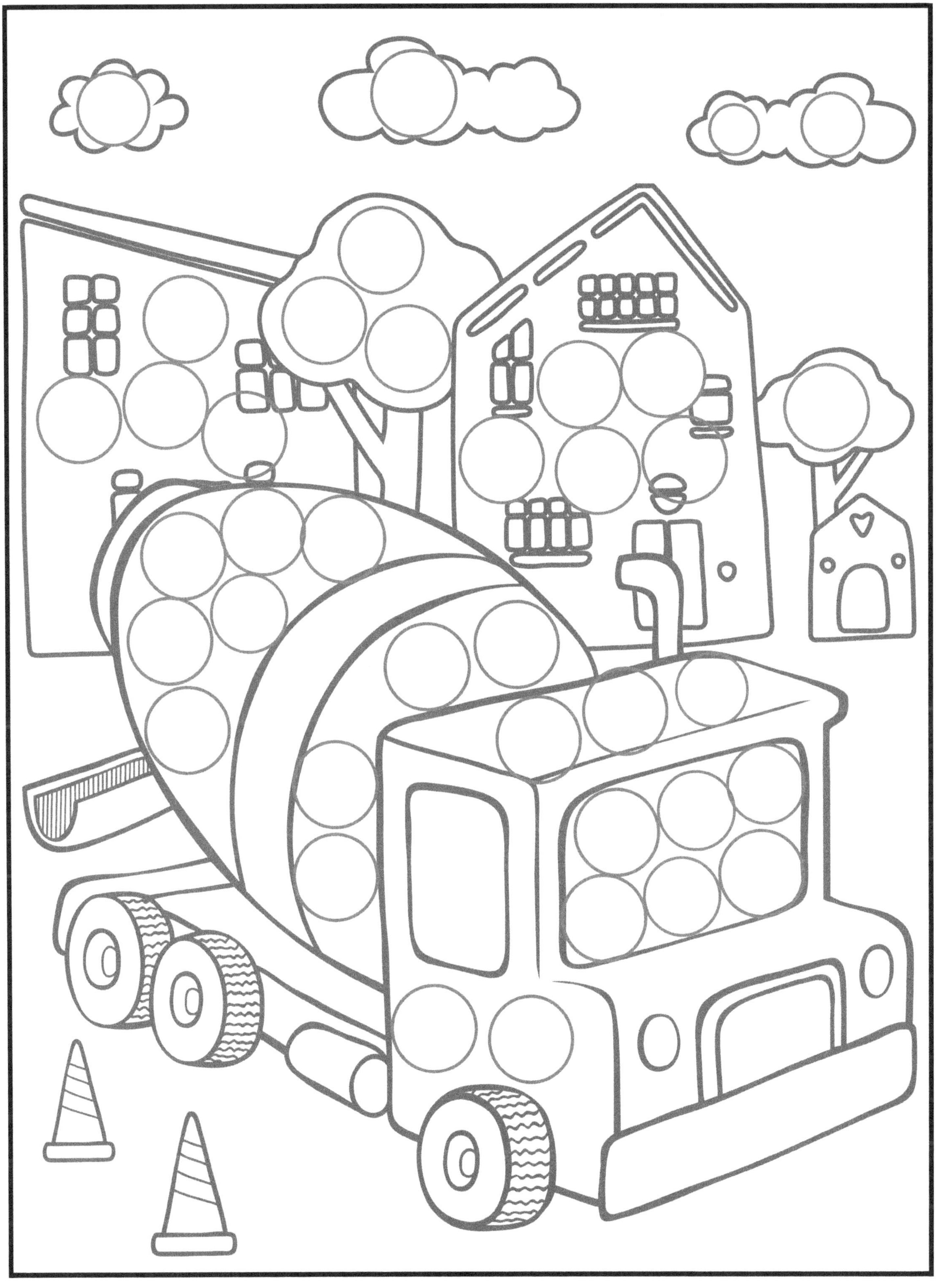

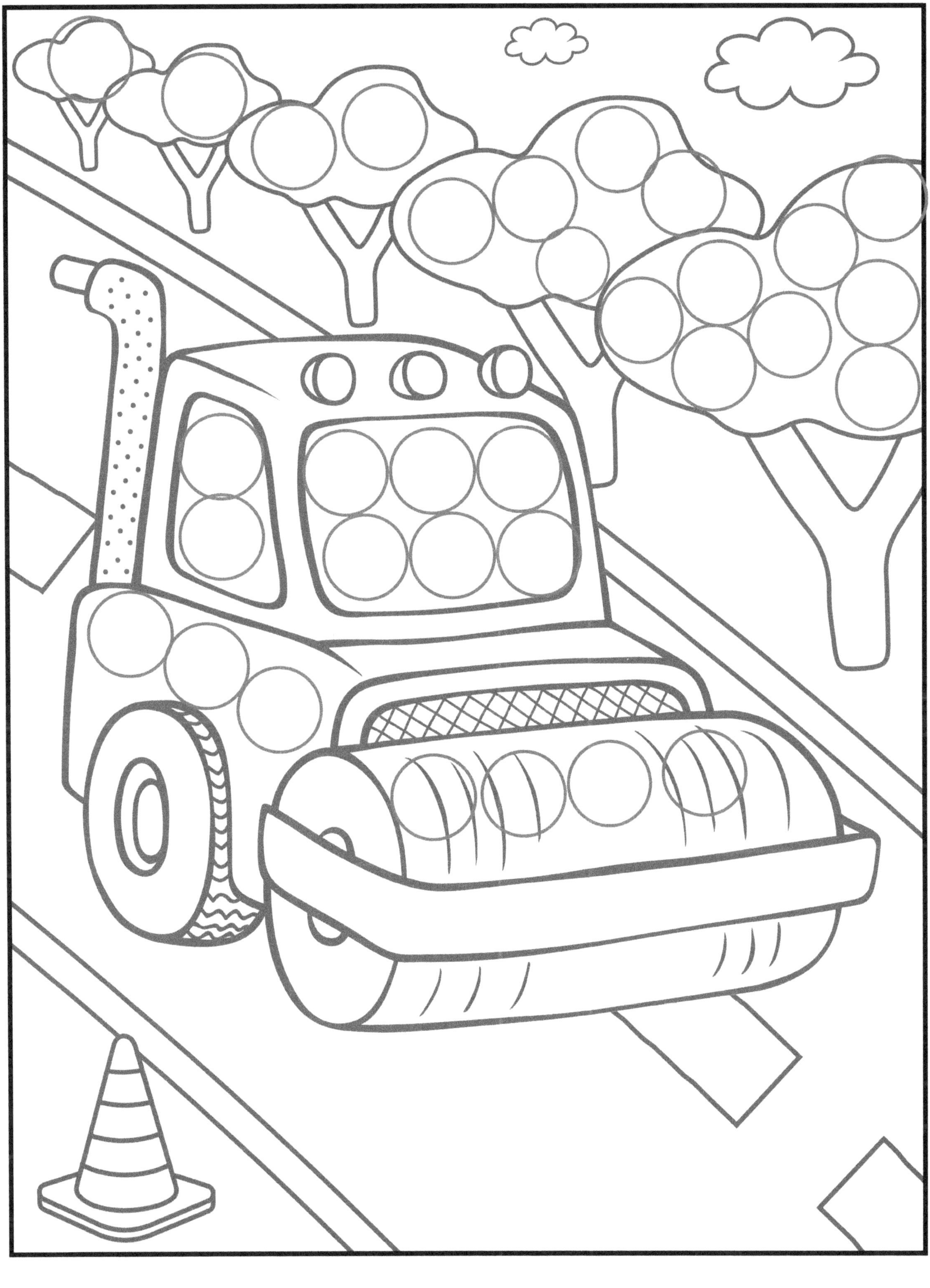

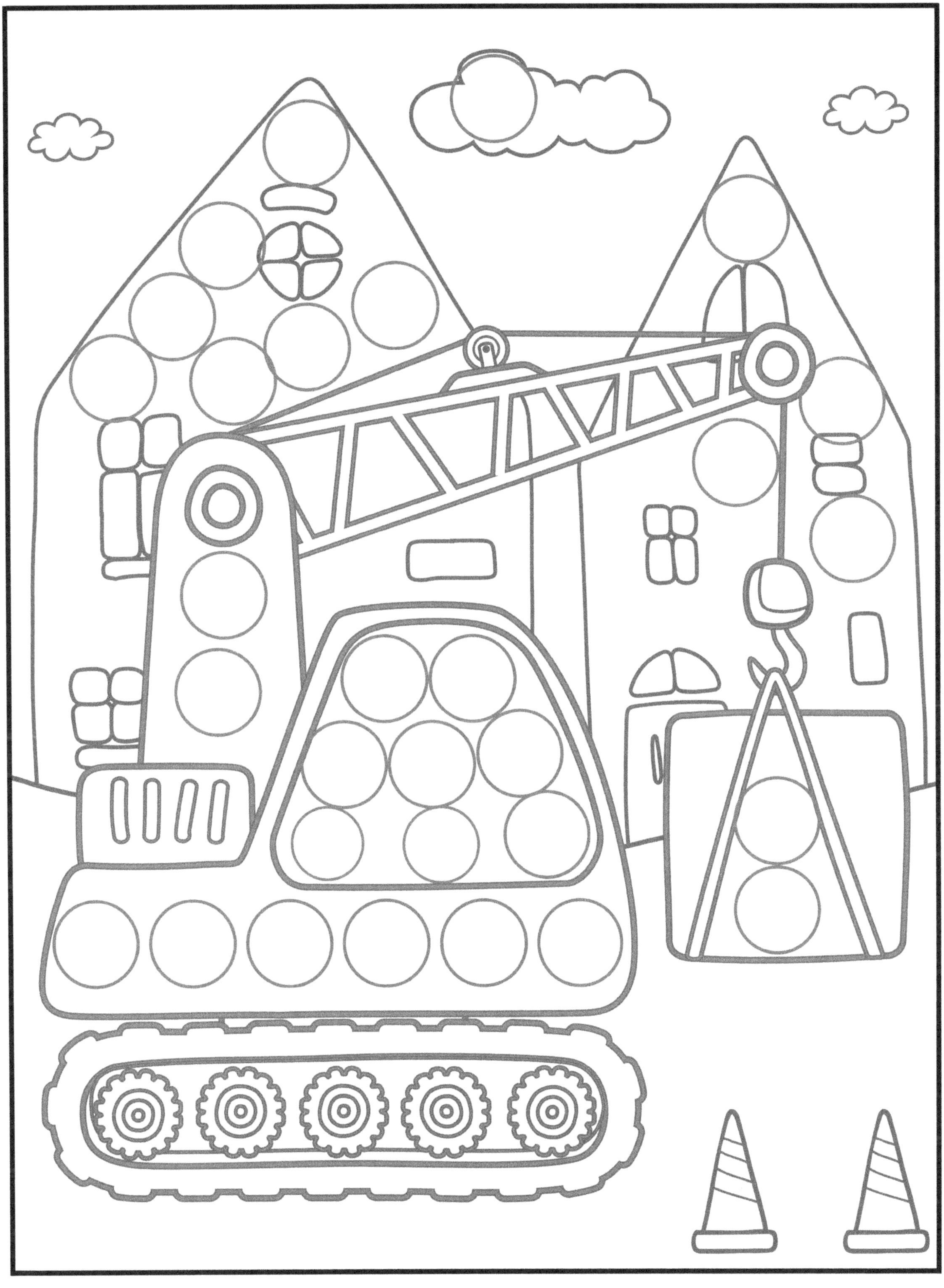

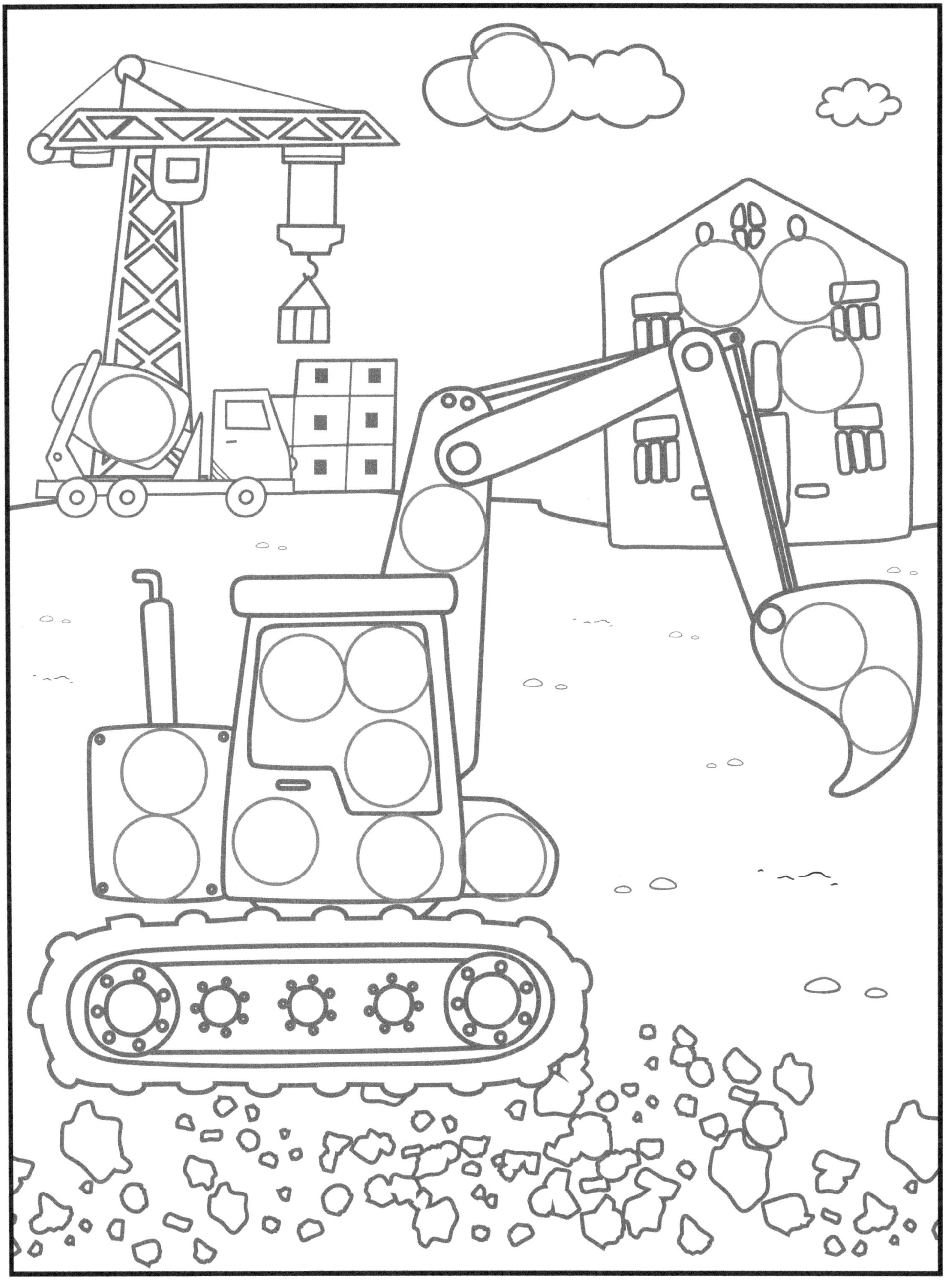

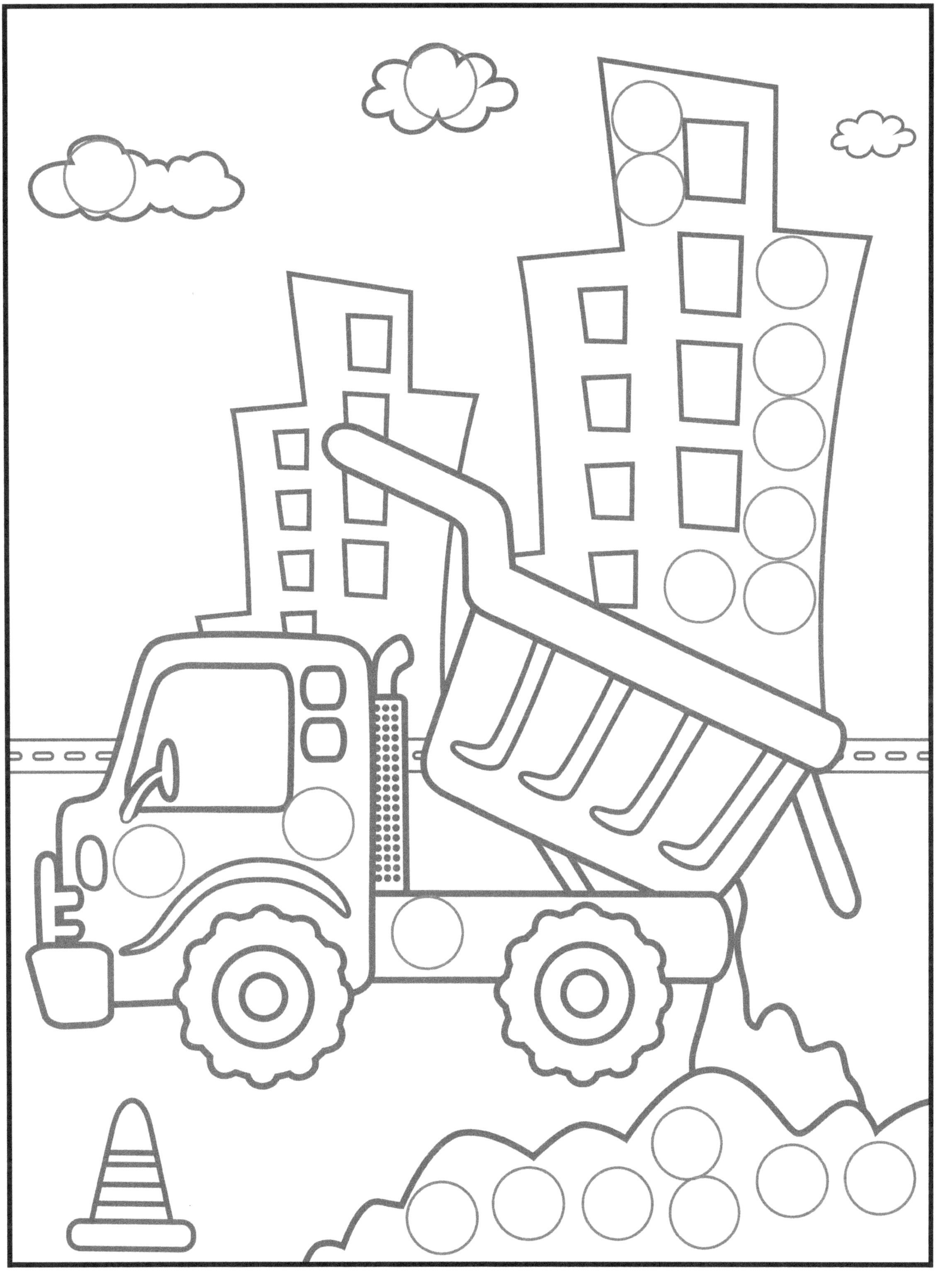

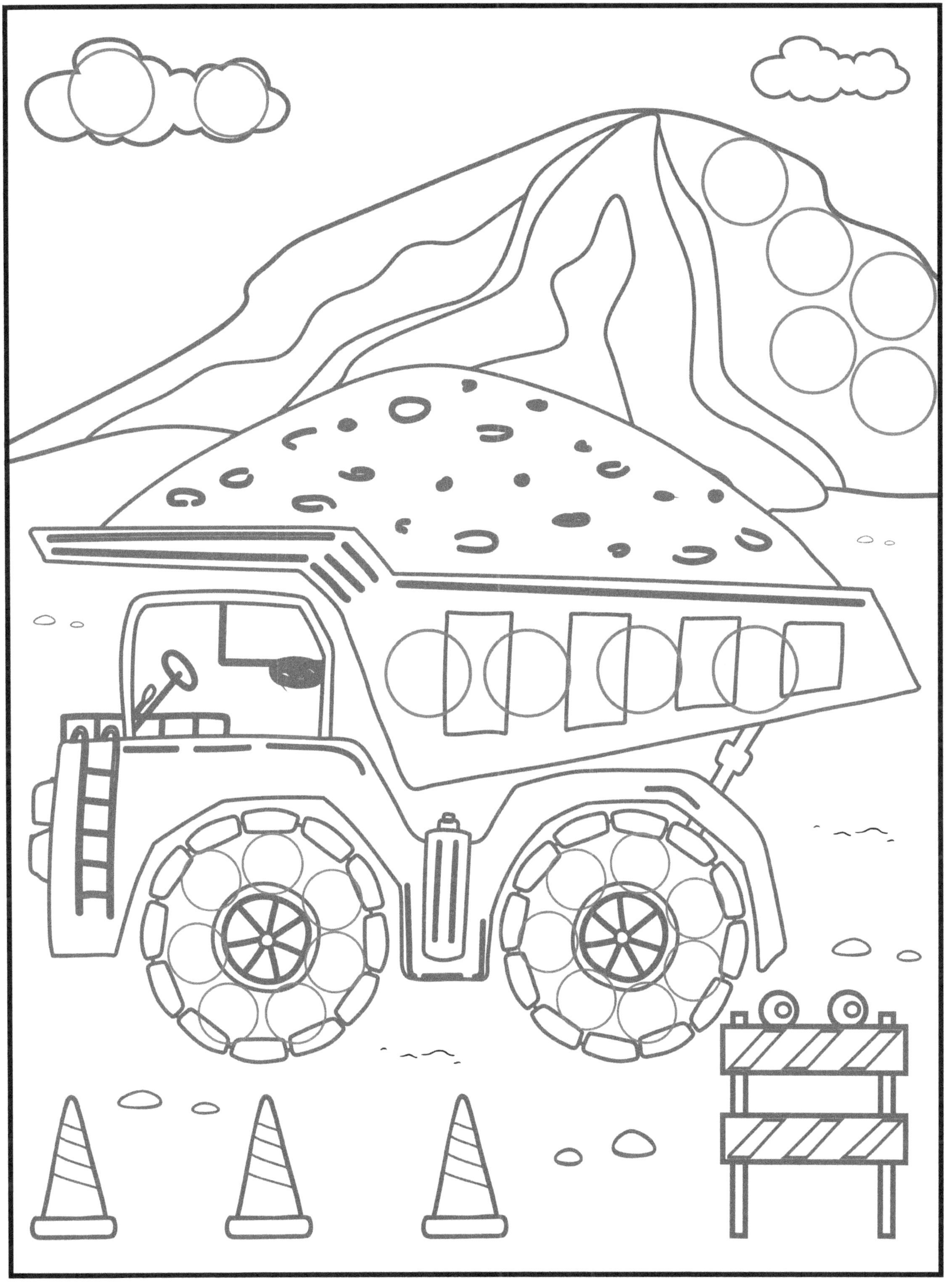

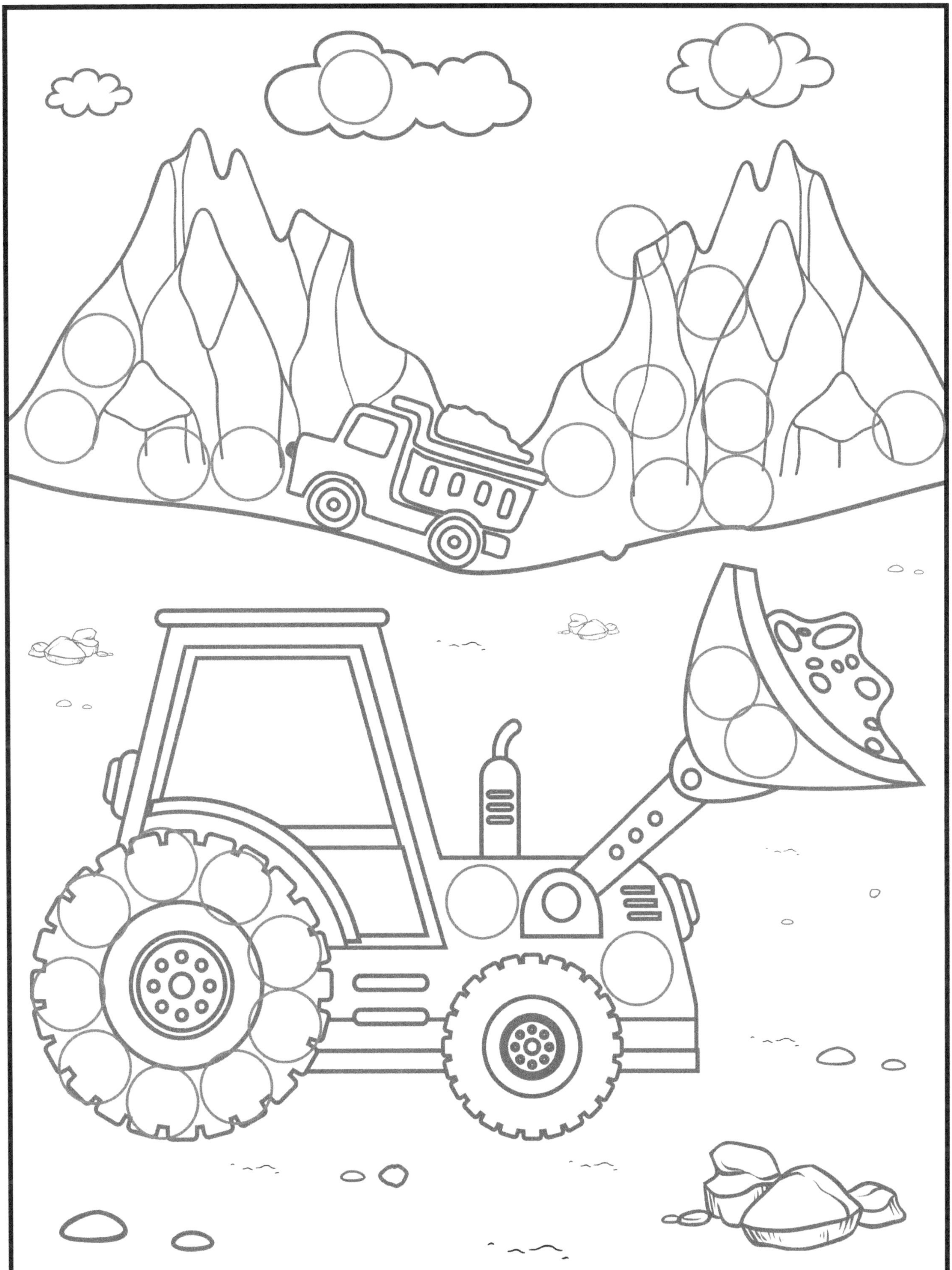

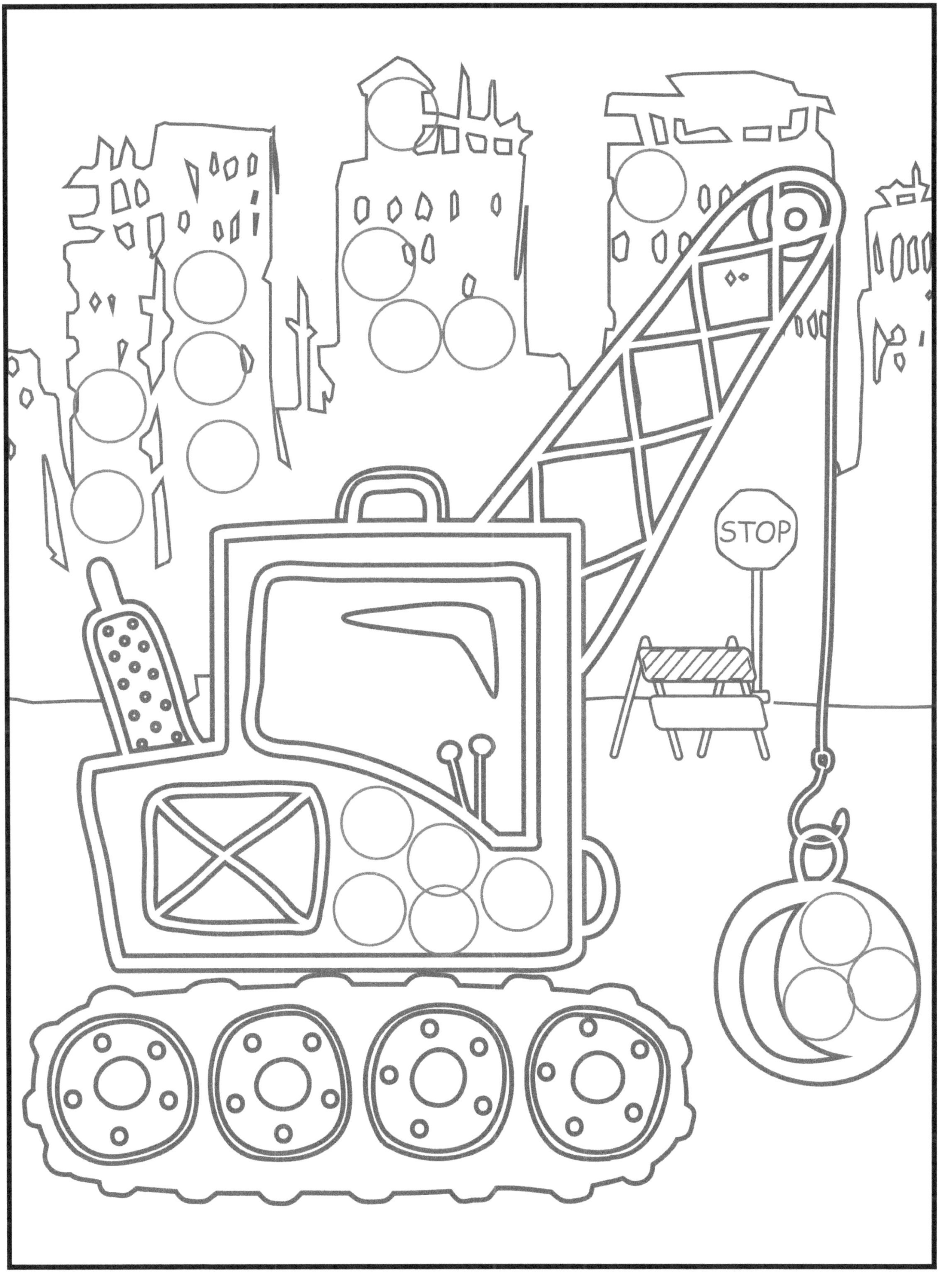
STOP

www.ingramcontent.com/pod-product-compliance
Lightning Source LLC
Chambersburg PA
CBHW081420220526
45467CB00009B/2760
9798718316278